Martin Luther

by Simonetta Carr

with Illustrations by Troy Howell

REFORMATION HERITAGE BOOKS

Grand Rapids, Michigan

Martin Luther
© 2016 by Simonetta Carr

Cover artwork by Troy Howell

For additional artwork by Troy, see pages 9, 11, 15, 27, 29, 31, 33, 41, 45, 51, and 53
.

Reformation Heritage Books
2965 Leonard St. NE
Grand Rapids, MI 49525
616-977-0889 / Fax: 616-285-3246
e-mail: orders@heritagebooks.org
website: www.heritagebooks.org

Printed in the United States of America
16 17 18 19 20 21/10 9 8 7 6 5 4 3 2 1

Library of Congress Cataloging-in-Publication Data

Names: Carr, Simonetta, author. | Howell, Troy, illustrator.
Title: Martin Luther / by Simonetta Carr ; with illustrations by Troy Howell.
Description: Grand Rapids, Michigan : Reformation Heritage Books, 2016. |
    Series: Christian biographies for young readers
Identifiers: LCCN 2016038487 | ISBN 9781601784544 (hardcover : alk. paper)
Subjects: LCSH: Luther, Martin, 1483-1546—Juvenile literature. |
    Reformation—Germany—Biography—Juvenile literature.
Classification: LCC BR325 .C27 2016 | DDC 284.1092 [B] —dc23 LC record
    available at https://lccn.loc.gov/2016038487

For additional Reformed literature, request a free book list from Reformation Heritage Books at the above address.

CHRISTIAN BIOGRAPHIES FOR YOUNG READERS

This series introduces children to important people in the Christian tradition. Parents and schoolteachers alike will welcome the excellent educational value it provides for students, while the quality of the publication and the artwork make each volume a keepsake for generations to come. Furthermore, the books in the series go beyond the simple story of someone's life by teaching young readers the historical and theological relevance of each character.

AVAILABLE VOLUMES OF THE SERIES
John Calvin
Augustine of Hippo
John Owen
Athanasius
Lady Jane Grey
Anselm of Canterbury
John Knox
Jonathan Edwards
Marie Durand
Martin Luther

SOME ANTICIPATED VOLUMES
Peter Martyr Vermigli
...and more

Table of Contents

A map of Europe during Luther's life. You may want to use it to follow his travels. At that time, Germany was part of the Holy Roman Empire and was composed of about 350 small provinces, each with its own ruler. The map shows only the borders of the Holy Roman Empire and the cities that are mentioned in this story.

Introduction

It took only a few months for ninety-five troubling questions to stir a nation, and only a few years for them to shake a continent, changing the course not only of the Western church but also of world history. Yet when Martin Luther wrote them, he wanted to discuss some matters about sin and repentance with only his students and other professors. To his surprise, his questions were quickly copied, translated, and distributed from city to city, awakening similar concerns in many other people.

Today, Martin Luther is considered one of the most influential leaders of the Protestant Reformation, and his words are still impacting Christians all over the world.

·IACTA·CVRAM·TVAM·IN·DOMINVM·ET· ·IPSE·TE·ENVTRIET·

Martin Luther

CHAPTER ONE

From Law Student to Monk

Martin was born on November 10, 1483, in the small town of Eisleben in central Germany. His father, Hans, was a farmer's son. Soon after Martin's birth, Hans moved his family to nearby Mansfeld so he could work in the copper mines. Extracting metal from under the ground was a hard job, but Hans worked diligently and soon became a supervisor. Martin always considered Mansfeld his hometown.

PAINTINGS BY LUCAS CRANACH THE ELDER, HELD AT WARTBURG-STIFTUNG EISENACH. PHOTO BY ULRICH KNEISE.

Hans Luther   Margaritha Luther

Martin had seven siblings, but only four lived to be adults: three sisters and his favorite brother Jacob, who was seven years younger. As a child, Jacob always asked to sit next to Martin at meals and was happy to play with other children only when Martin was there. Hans and his wife, Margaritha, were strict by today's standards. Later in life, Martin understood they had meant well.

Since Martin liked to study, Hans decided to prepare him to be a lawyer, which was a respectable job and not as exhausting as working in a mine. Hans was willing to make many sacrifices to reach that goal. At age fourteen, when Martin finished his basic studies at the local school, Hans sent him to study in nearby towns, arranging for his stay with relatives or other families. Martin returned home only for short visits.

School rules were harsh. If the children misbehaved, didn't study, or spoke German instead of Latin, the teachers would beat them with a rod. The worst student had to wear a sign around his neck. Students had to learn Latin because it was an important language. It was used for legal documents and was spoken by educated people all over Europe.

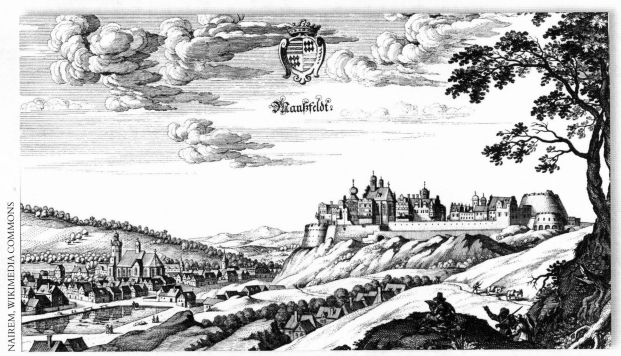

Seventeenth-century Mansfeld, engraving by Matthäus Merian, 1690

Sometimes students sang door-to-door to ask people to support their studies, usually by donating food. The stern school rules, however, had made Martin and his friends so fearful that when a man called "in a boorish voice" to offer them sausages, the boys ran away in fright and hid until the man managed to reassure them. Much later, Martin explained that we often act in a similar way when we don't believe God's loving promises. "We are afraid of a sausage, and we even fear those who wish us the best."

In 1501 Martin was admitted into the University of Erfurt, one of the best in the country. He studied hard and graduated with excellence in four years, the shortest time possible. In his free time, he liked to sing and play music with his friends, who were an important part of his life. He learned to sing very well and to play both the lute and the flute.

An ancient lute

Martin and his friends ran away in fright from a man who wanted to offer them sausages.

In the summer of 1505, just before entering his final course of studies, Martin paid a visit to his family. It was a difficult time for the region. Erfurt had been struck by the plague, a serious illness that had killed so many people that entire cities were left empty. Even some of Martin's friends and teachers had died. Martin was worried about death because he thought he had not done enough to please God.

On his way back to college, he was caught in a massive thunderstorm that filled him with terror. Fearful at the thought of having to face God, he cried, "Help me, St. Anne! I will become a monk." At that time, Jesus and God were both seen as angry judges of sinners, so people looked for protection from saints—godly people who had died. It was also common to add a promise to do something good in return for the saint's protection.

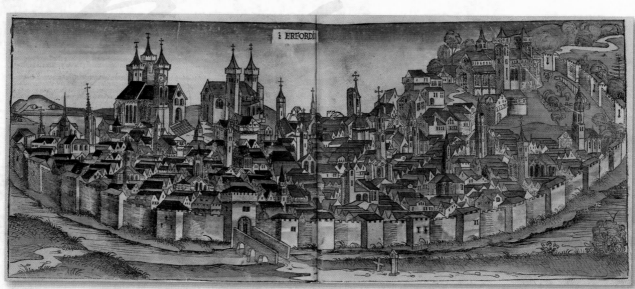

WOODCUT FROM LIBER CHRONACORUM, 1493, WIKIMEDIA COMMONS

Fifteenth-Century Erfurt

On his way back to the college, Martin was caught in a massive thunderstorm that filled him with terror.

CHAPTER TWO

In Search of Peace with God

Once Martin arrived safely in Erfurt, he considered carefully his promise to St. Anne. Even by church standards, he didn't have to keep it because obedience to parents was more important than keeping a hasty pledge. By becoming a monk, Martin would have shattered his father's dreams.

JON BERNDT OLSEN

Porch at the Augustinian monastery in Erfurt

Still, he persisted in his decision. It was not the first time this thought had crossed his mind. Like most people at that time, Martin thought that living like a monk was the surest way to please God. Monks live together in places called monasteries and devote most of their time to prayer and meditation. (Women who do this are called nuns, and they live in convents.)

As required of new monks, Martin gave away all his possessions—his lute, his books, his eating utensils, and even his clothes, because monks wore only a tunic and a cape. He then entered one of the strictest monastic orders in Germany. Seven times a day, including once in the middle of the night, he prayed and sang together with the other monks. Speaking was only allowed at certain times, and laughing was forbidden. Martin obeyed all the rules diligently. In fact, he did more than what was required.

In spite of these efforts, he was never sure God could accept him. He tried to find an answer in the Bible. At that time, priests, monks, and nuns had the best access to Bibles, and the monastery was the first place where Martin could seriously study this book. He studied it more earnestly than his fellow monks, eager to find peace of mind. Instead, he kept reading about God's anger against sinners and didn't see a way to escape it.

Confessing his sins to a senior monk gave him only brief comfort. Sometimes he returned a few minutes after confession because a new sinful thought had passed through his mind. Frustrated by his insistence, his superiors told him to confess only big sins. To Martin, this was impossible. The Bible teaches that God hates every sin, big or small.

In 1510 Martin was sent to Rome as a traveling companion for a senior monk. Rome—the capital of the Roman Catholic Church—was known as the Holy City. Tens of thousands of pilgrims walked there every year, even from long distances, hoping to gain God's forgiveness and approval. Martin had similar hopes.

It was the longest trip Martin had taken. He walked almost one thousand miles in about two months. Once he arrived, he visited the seven most important churches in the city all in one day, while fasting. He also climbed a special stairway of twenty-eight marble steps (known as the Holy Steps) on his knees. With each step, he said the Lord's Prayer.

According to the Roman Catholic Church, this practice helped people earn God's forgiveness for themselves or for others. Martin climbed on behalf of his grandparents. When he arrived at the top of the stairs, someone rushed him away to make room for others. Few of the religious people in Rome seemed to have sincere respect for God. Religious practices such as climbing the Holy Steps seemed to be more of a business than sincere worship. Martin wondered if the church's promises of blessing for doing these things were really based on truth.

DAN ZELAZO

These stairs, called the Holy Steps, were supposedly the steps of Pilate's palace, which Jesus climbed before being condemned to death. The paintings on the walls were added after Luther's visit to Rome.

When he arrived on the top of the Holy Steps, he wondered, "Who knows if it's really so?"

Soon after Martin's return to Erfurt, his superior sent him to the German city of Wittenberg (pronounced *VIT-ten-berg*) to complete his education and teach university courses. He tried to refuse. He didn't feel more qualified than his fellow monks. Besides, teaching was a hard job, and Martin was afraid he would not live long under the strain. His superior was not impressed by his excuses. Death was not a problem, he said, because God had plenty of work for good teachers in heaven.

In 1512, at the age of twenty-nine, Martin became a professor of Bible studies. From this time on, everyone called him Dr. Luther. As it was customary, he took an oath promising to teach the Scriptures faithfully. In 1516, when many copies of the New Testament were published for the first time in the original Greek language, he was able to obtain one. This helped him to understand the Bible much better and teach more accurately.

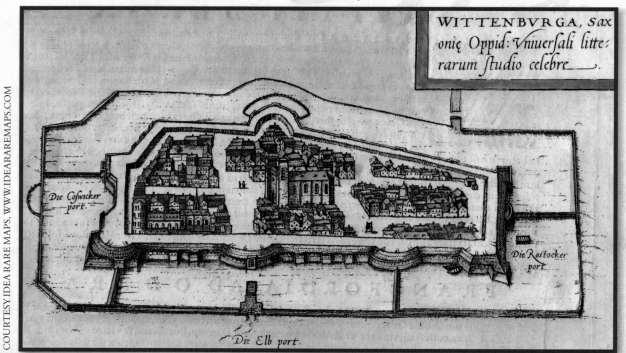

Detail of the City of Wittenberg, from Civitates Orbis Terrarum by Georg Braun and Franz Hogenberg, edited in Cologne, Germany, 1572

CHAPTER THREE

A Powerful List

ISTOCK

Pope Leo X

*I*n the meantime, the head of the Roman Catholic Church, Pope Leo X, was having financial problems. Like other popes before him, he wanted to rebuild Rome's Cathedral of St. Peter into the greatest church building ever seen, but he had already spent too much money and still needed the equivalent of millions of dollars. He had, however, a way to get this money quickly: he could create more indulgences for sale.

Indulgences were official declarations that people could buy to give themselves and their loved ones a shorter stay in purgatory. The church taught that purgatory was a place where sinners went after they died to be "purged" of

Johann Tetzel

their sins before they went on to heaven. The stay in purgatory was not at all pleasant, so people were eager to find a way out.

The sale of indulgences had turned into a business. The pope signed them, and the bishops or archbishops (leaders in the Roman Catholic Church) sold them and sent the pope a large portion of the profits. At that time, an archbishop in Germany needed money to expand his properties, so he worked with Pope Leo and put a clever preacher, Johann Tetzel, in charge of marketing.

Tetzel traveled from town to town preaching about the benefits of indulgences. "Have mercy upon your dead parents," he said. "Whoever has an indulgence has salvation. Everything else is of no avail." To help people remember this teaching, he created a jingle and sang it wherever he went: "As soon as the coin in the coffer rings, the soul from purgatory springs!"

All over Germany, people rushed to buy indulgences. The price of the indulgence depended on how many years out of purgatory the buyer was purchasing, but it was always cheaper than a trip to Rome. Not everyone liked this business. Frederick "the Wise," ruler of Saxony (Wittenberg's region), forbade this type of sale, but many of his citizens still traveled to other regions to buy indulgences.

By that time, Luther was preaching regularly in the city church and supervising ten monasteries. Because of this, he was especially concerned that indulgences gave his people false hope. Besides, was the church authorized to decrease a punishment decided by God?

RENÉ, FLICKR

A treasure chest used to collect the money from the sale of indulgences

19

The church in Wittenberg where Luther is said to have posted the Ninety-Five Theses was attached to Frederick's castle. The original church door was destroyed by fire in the eighteenth century.

RENÉ, FLICKR

At first, Luther expressed these concerns in his sermons. On October 31, 1517, he compiled them into a set of ninety-five questions (also known as theses, pronounced *THEE-seez*) and included them in a respectful letter to the archbishop who had ordered the sales. He probably nailed a copy to the church's main door, which served as a bulletin board, inviting his students and other professors to an open discussion.

He didn't mean to protest. He thought the problems with indulgences were just a big misunderstanding and that the pope would be glad to remedy the situation.

...uther compiled a set of ninety-five questions about the sale of indulgences and other matters of sin and repentance.

The theses were written in Latin and were not meant for everyone. Someone, however, translated them into German, printed them, and sent them throughout the country, where they went viral.

German rulers read them with great interest. They had been complaining for some time about the large amount of money that was flowing out of Germany into Italy to support a foreign ruler (the pope), and were happy that someone in the church wanted to discuss these problems.

When the pope received a copy of the theses, he wasn't too concerned. He asked his official theologian to write Luther and correct his mistakes. This theologian reminded Luther that, according to Roman Catholic Church laws, a pope could not be judged or deposed, even if he led people "by crowds into the possession of hell." Luther was shocked. "I think that everyone in Rome has gone crazy," he wrote to a friend.

The pope sent one of his officers to convince Luther to take back what he had written. If the monk refused, the officer had orders to bring him to Rome. Luther met the officer in the city of Augsburg and told him he had simply tried to keep his promise to teach the Scriptures faithfully. When he discovered the officer was ready to take him to Rome, he left by night and returned to Wittenberg.

Soon after this, the German emperor died, and seven princes (including Frederick the Wise) prepared to elect a new ruler. Frederick, who liked Luther, made his candidate promise he would give Luther a fair trial in Germany. In June 1519, Frederick's choice became emperor under the name of Charles V.

Under Frederick's protection, Luther continued to study the Scriptures, especially those he found most difficult. He had always been troubled by Romans 1:17, which teaches that in the gospel "is the righteousness of God revealed from faith to faith." Luther didn't understand. If God's righteousness is perfect and no man can reach perfection, how can the gospel that reveals it be good news? "I hated that phrase—the righteousness of God," Luther said. In fact, he hated God for demanding that righteousness.

He continued to study the Scriptures and the writings of earlier Christians. He also kept praying and discussing these

COURTESY NATIONAL ART GALLERY, ROSENWALD COLLECTION

Frederick the Wise

things with other teachers. More and more, he realized that "the righteousness of God" in this verse is not a righteousness God demands, but a righteousness God gives in Jesus Christ. He was overjoyed. He knew that it was only "by the mercy of God" that he could come to this understanding.

He felt he "had entered paradise itself through open gates." Little did he realize at this time that the doctrine of justification by faith alone would become the foundation of what later would be called the Protestant faith.

It was apparently in this tower that Luther received a new understanding of Romans 1:17.

GILLES DESPINS

Luther continued to study and write. One of his most important books was *To the Christian Nobility of the German Nation*, where he encouraged Charles V and his nobles to support a reform of the church. He explained that ordinary Christians play an important role in the church. If the church is not preaching the gospel, Christians can't wait for the pope to make changes, just like citizens can't wait for the mayor to put out a city fire. They must take matters into their own hands. Four thousand copies of this book sold out in a few days after its publication.

He addressed another book, *On the Freedom of a Christian*, to the pope as a peaceful explanation of his thoughts. If Christians are accepted by God just because of what Christ did for them, he explained, they are free to love others and to obey God's laws out of love and not out of fear, without looking for other ways to get God's favor.

Charles V

Far from being convinced by Luther, Leo sent out an official notice threatening to exclude the monk from the Roman Catholic Church—the only type of church in Western Europe in those days. He had sixty days to repent.

By the time the notice reached Wittenberg, Luther had thought carefully about his beliefs and was convinced he was standing on God's Word. When he received the notice, he burned it publicly by the city gates. This gesture made his break with Rome final.

Title page of Leo X's Papal Bull for Luther's Excommunication, 1520

HIP / ART RESOURCE, NY

When Luther received the papal notice of excommunication, he burned it publicly.

At this point, Charles V, a devout Roman Catholic, could easily send his men to arrest Luther. Instead, to keep his promise to Frederick, he invited Luther to an upcoming meeting (or Diet, pronounced *DEE-at*) in the city of Worms (pronounced *verms*), where the monk could be tried by German rulers. Luther's friends begged him not to go. They were sure he would be sentenced to death. Luther was not ready to disobey the emperor. He also hoped to be heard by impartial judges.

On April 2, Luther started his two-week journey to Worms, escorted by Frederick's guards. As he traveled, he realized how many people were grateful for his writings. In Erfurt, he was greeted by a triumphal procession and showered with gifts. At Worms, he was cheered by a crowd of about two thousand people. A Roman Catholic officer reported that nine out of ten people were shouting in support of Luther, and the other one was shouting against the pope.

As Luther traveled, he realized how many people were grateful for his writings.

CHAPTER FOUR

A Reluctant Rebel

The emperor had planned to devote only a short time to Luther. He instructed his secretary to point to a pile of Luther's books and to ask the monk if he was ready to take back, or retract, what he had written. Luther was surprised. He had hoped to have a chance to discuss his ideas. Speaking softly, he asked for an extra night to pray and formulate an answer. The emperor and princes were surprised that a man who had boldly attacked the pope would be so timid, but they allowed him another day.

GILLES DESPINS

The Cathedral of Worms, where the imperial meeting took place

This gave Luther time to prayerfully compose, memorize, and rehearse his answer since he was not allowed to read it. When he was called back to the meeting, he spoke loudly and without fear. He made a distinction between the harsh tone and language of some of his writings, which was not fit for a professor or monk, and the truth the books contained. He was more than willing to retract any disrespectful sentence, but could not retract the truth.

Luther explained why he couldn't retract what he had written.

The imperial secretary didn't care for distinctions. Was Luther ready to retract all his books, not just some portions? Finally, Luther replied, "Unless I am convinced by the testimony of the Scriptures and by clear reason (for I do not trust either in the pope or in councils alone, since it is well known that they have often erred and contradicted themselves), I am bound by the Scriptures I have quoted, and my conscience is captive to the Word of God. I cannot and I will not retract anything, since it is neither right nor safe to go against conscience."

The next day, Charles told the council Luther should be condemned. At the same time, he kept his promise and let him leave unharmed. Frederick, however, didn't want to take chances and planned a fake kidnapping to save Luther's life.

Luther was aware of the plan. When he arrived at the appointed place, he told the imperial escort he didn't need them anymore and kept only two friends with him. Soon after that, a group of Frederick's soldiers attacked Luther's wagon in a narrow valley, tied the monk, and made him walk behind one of their horses.

A group of soldiers attacked Luther's wagon in a narrow valley.

CHAPTER FIVE

Starting a Reformation

Albrecht Dürer
LIBRARY OF CONGRESS

As soon as they were out of sight, the soldiers untied Luther, mounted him on a horse, and took him by long detours to Frederick's castle of Wartburg (pronounced *VART-burg*) in an isolated forest area.

The story of Luther's kidnapping was related all over Germany. People were shocked and distressed. The famous painter Albrecht Dürer wrote in his diary, "O God, if Luther is dead, who will in future so clearly proclaim to us the holy gospel? O my God, what might he not still have written in ten or twenty years!"

Wartburg Castle

GILLES DESPINS

Dürer didn't know that Luther was alive and well and still writing. Mostly, Luther used this time to translate the New Testament from Greek into German, completing his work in a few months. The translation was a great success. Even though books were very expensive compared to today's prices, and even though the pope had forbidden Roman Catholics from reading Luther's works, three thousand copies of this New Testament sold within a few days.

Luther's room in the Wartburg Castle, where Luther spent most of his time writing and translating

GILLES DESPINS

Luther disguised as Junker Jörg

One of Luther's opponents was so surprised that he wrote, "Shoemakers and women and every kind of unlearned person, whoever of them were Lutherans and had somehow learned German letters, read it most eagerly as the font of all truth. And by reading and rereading it they committed it to memory and so carried the book around with them in their bosoms." That was exactly what Luther wanted.

Luther, now an outlaw, disguised himself as a knight by growing out his hair, having a beard, and dressing for the part. If anyone saw him, he called himself Junker Jörg (pronounced *YOON-kar yerg*), meaning "young lord George." The man in charge of the castle made sure Luther's stay was pleasant. Still, Luther felt isolated and exiled, like John, the author of the book of Revelation, on the small island of Patmos. Luther referred to the castle as "the kingdom of the birds" because it was populated mostly by birds, not by people.

In the meantime, in Wittenberg, two of Luther's friends, Phillip Melanchthon and Andreas Karlstadt, worked to reorganize the church according to Luther's teachings. For example, they used German—not Latin—in all church services and changed the way the Lord's Supper was served to help Christians understand its meaning.

Not everyone was ready to change. Some were anxious about leaving traditions they had held all their lives. When Melanchthon asked Luther what to do, Luther suggested to go slowly and to keep preaching the gospel. Only the gospel—the good news of Christ's life, death, and resurrection—has the power to change hearts.

Karlstadt and a few others, instead, wanted to make changes mandatory and to impose them by force. Some went as far as smashing statues, burning paintings, and injuring some monks. There was so much violence that the city council begged Luther to return.

Phillip Melanchthon

The drawbridge Luther crossed when he left the Wartburg Castle

GILLES DESPINS

Luther knew that leaving Wartburg would place his life in danger, but the situation in Wittenberg was too urgent. When he arrived, he was shocked to see the destruction that had taken place. He preached every day for a week, encouraging people to show charity and understanding toward each other. He explained that the gospel is a gift to be received, not a law to be enforced. "The matter should be left to God," he said. "His Word should do the work alone."

Not everyone agreed. Some, including Karlstadt, believed the Spirit could speak without God's Word. "With all his mouthing of the words 'Spirit, Spirit, Spirit,'" Luther said about Karlstadt, "he tears down the bridge, the path, the way, the ladder, and all the means by which the Spirit comes to you," which are the preaching of the gospel and the sacraments.

Luther preaching

Luther was shocked when he saw the destruction in Wittenberg.

In spite of his efforts, Luther could not stop the violence that sprang up later when some peasants, tired of being abused by their lords, started a rebellion. Luther wrote a message to both lords and peasants. He blamed the lords, who had been unfair, and told the peasants to be moderate in their demands.

He realized the seriousness of the rebellion while preaching in a small town outside of Wittenberg. There, he found himself in the middle of a violent riot that forced him to stop his sermon and run to safety. He then wrote an attachment to his previous message, explaining that even if the peasants were right, lawless violence is always wrong. Besides, the riots and chaos were hurting the weak more than the powerful. The violence had to be stopped.

By the time his advice was published, however, the rebellion had turned into a war. To quench it, the rulers' armies killed about one hundred thousand peasants, both violent and nonviolent, and burned many of their properties. Luther's new publication made it look as though he approved of this massacre. It was a trying time, as Roman Catholics blamed him for the killing and many peasants became disappointed in him.

CHAPTER SIX

Raising a Family

Luther's writings were changing Europe in other ways too. For example, many priests, monks, and nuns started to leave the Roman Catholic Church secretly. Leaving a convent was more difficult for nuns than for monks because it was harder for women to start a new life. In 1523, when nine nuns arrived in Wittenberg, the leaders of Luther's church tried to find them good homes. Many of the women got married.

GILLES DESPINS

Statue of Katherina Van Bora in Wittenberg

One of these nuns, Katherina von Bora, suffered a great disappointment when a man she had hoped to marry broke the engagement without giving a reason. Luther gave her other suggestions, but she didn't like them. Instead, she said she would be willing to marry Luther!

At first, Luther thought it was a ridiculous idea, but some of his friends encouraged him to do it. After all, he had been teaching for some time about the benefits of marriage. He sought advice from his father, who was immediately thrilled. He had always wanted Luther to have a family. Luther was happy to finally please his father. The wedding was celebrated as soon as his parents could attend. The event made news everywhere—an ex-monk marrying an ex-nun!

Martin and Katherina learned to love and appreciate each other and worked well together. In 1527, when the plague struck Wittenberg, they both devoted their efforts to help others, even though the university studies were moved temporarily to another town. In fact, they even took some of the sick into their home. They knew they were putting their lives in danger but submitted to God's will, in life and in death. Their faith was put to a difficult test when their firstborn son, one-year old Hans, became ill. Thankfully, he soon recovered.

When the plague struck Wittenberg, Martin and Katherina devoted their efforts to help others,
even taking some of the sick into their home.

Luther believed that public officials, pastors, and anyone who had to take care of other people should not abandon their duty. "Put your trust in the Lord," he said in a sermon. "Do not forsake your neighbor." It was probably around this time that he wrote the famous hymn "A Mighty Fortress," a faith-filled song based on Psalm 46.

The plague ended in 1528. The Luther family survived. The stressful situation, however, weakened Katherina, who was pregnant with their second child. The baby, named Elisabeth, lived only eight months. Luther was surprised at the intensity of his pain, even though he believed the child was safe in heaven.

After Elisabeth's death, the Luthers had four more children—Magdalene, Martin, Paul, and Margaret. In 1529, when Martin's sister died, leaving her six children without a parent, Martin and Katherina added those little ones to their family.

Thankfully, John the Steadfast (who had taken the place of his brother Frederick the Wise) had allowed the Luthers free use of an old monastery, where they could raise their large family and take in guests.

Luther said he learned more about love and self-discipline in his family than he had ever learned in the monastery. He also appreciated the children's cheerful confidence in their parents as a good reminder of the trust all Christians should have in God.

Luther spent much time with his family. Music had an important place in the home.

Luther's house in Wittenberg
GILLES DESPINS

At home Luther spent much time teaching both his children and the students who stayed at his house. When he visited nearby villages, however, he realized there was still a great ignorance of the Scriptures. "All the people are supposed to be Christians, have been baptized, and receive the Holy Sacrament even though they do not know the Lord's Prayer, the Creed, or the Ten Commandments," he wrote. Even many pastors were not properly trained to teach.

To remedy this situation, he published a catechism as a teaching tool for pastors and parents and included instructions to fathers on how to hold daily family prayers. He also finished his translation of the entire Bible. It was not the first German translation of the Scriptures, but it was written in such a way that everyone could easily understand them.

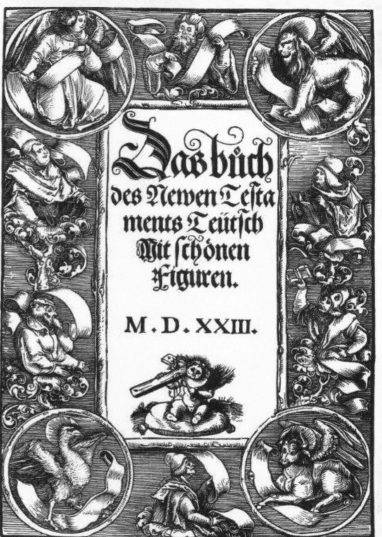

A reproduction of the title page of Luther's 1523 New Testament

It was also at home that Luther experienced the deepest sorrows. In 1542 Magdalene became very ill. As her sickness progressed, Luther explained that she might have to leave this world to be with God. She was not afraid. Luther stayed by her side until the end, when she died in his arms. Katherina stood at a distance, too distressed to come near. Luther's pain was even greater than when he had lost his first daughter, because he had come to know Magdalene and enjoy her company for thirteen years.

By this time, Luther was fifty-nine years old. He felt old and tired and thought he had done enough in this life. At the same time, people still needed his help. In 1546, at the age of sixty-three, he traveled by horse and carriage to his native town of Eisleben, where he had been called to restore the peace among two rulers. Katherine was not happy to see her husband leave. He had not been feeling well, and she thought he was not strong enough to travel.

ERICH LESSING / ART RESOURCE, NY

A painting by Lucas Cranach the Elder, probably depicting Magdalene Luther. Musée du Louvre.

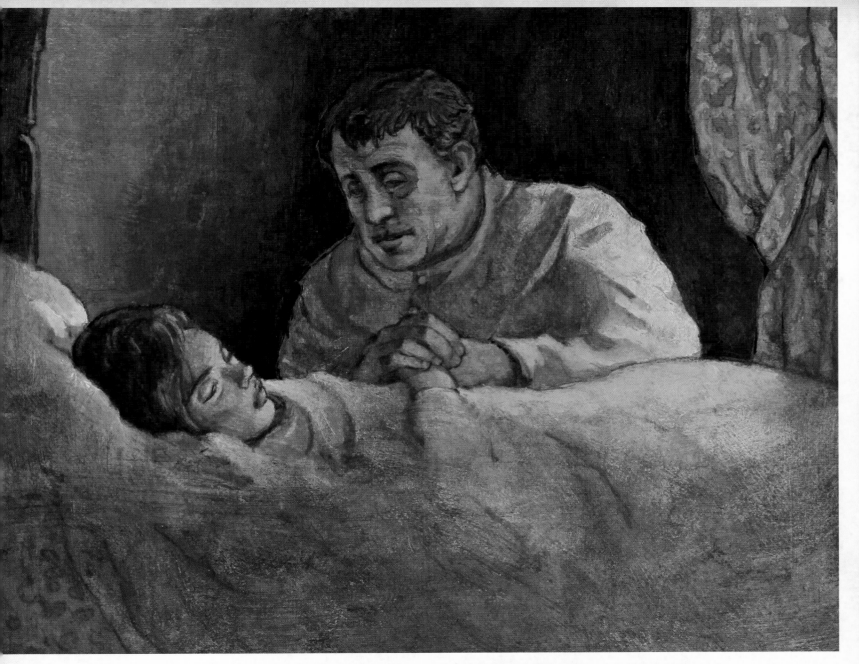

As Magdalene's sickness continued to worsen, Luther explained that she might
have to leave this world to be with God.

CHAPTER SEVEN

Ready to Die in the Lord

Luther's deathbed

During the trip, Luther had a series of heart attacks. The last one came on February 17. Soon, it was obvious that he was going to die. One of his assistants asked him, "Are you ready to die trusting in your Lord Jesus Christ and to confess the doctrine which you have taught in his name?" Luther replied, "Yes." That was his final word.

Luther died surrounded by his sons and friends. After the funeral, his body was taken back to Wittenberg. The wagon that bore the coffin was followed by a long procession, which kept growing as bells were tolled in each village on the way. Finally, Luther was buried beneath the pulpit of the Castle Church, where he had preached many times before.

The wagon that bore Luther's coffin was followed by a long procession.

All the writings by Luther that have been passed down to us are collected in about one hundred large volumes. His Bible and catechisms have remained a foundation of the German church for centuries. What's more, his translation of the Bible is considered important for the development of the German language.

His greatest contribution, however, has been his uncompromising emphasis on the free promise of the gospel that we receive by faith alone. While many others attacked the abuses and corruption of the church and of the pope, Luther went to the root of the problem, which is in man's sinful heart, a problem that only God can solve. Another great Reformer, John Calvin, wrote after Luther's death, "We regard him as a remarkable apostle of Christ, through whose work and ministry, most of all, the purity of the Gospel has been restored in our time."

GILLES DESPINS

A statue of Luther as part of the Reformation monument in Worms

Did you know?

- Luther's last name at birth was Luder. When he moved to Wittenberg, he preferred to spell it *Luther,* as a wordplay on the Greek *eleutherius,* which means "free man."

- Martin Luther and his brother Jacob stayed friends all their lives and visited often. Apparently, Jacob was with Martin when Frederick's soldiers staged the attack and kidnapping. He was also in the funeral procession from Eisleben to Wittenberg and helped to comfort Katherina and the children.

- When he started to protect Luther, Frederick was a devout Roman Catholic and had a huge collection of relics. Relics are objects that people believe once belonged to Jesus, Mary, or some saint. For example, Frederick had a straw that allegedly came from Jesus's manger and a stick that supposedly came from Moses's burning bush. Most of the time, there was no truth in these claims. By the end of his life, however, Frederick had given up his relics collection.

- In Luther's time, diseases were made worse by poor sanitation and diet. In his letters to the sick, Luther recommends doctors and medicines along with prayer, because God uses these means. At the same time, he recognized that our state of mind has a lot to do with our health. He agreed with the saying, "Good cheer is half the battle." To those who were discouraged and couldn't find this good cheer, he recommended the company and support of other Christians. "The solitude of monks and nuns was an invention of the devil," he said. "Christ did not wish people to remain alone and so he gathered them into the church."

Another remedy against discouragement is activity. "The human heart must have something to do. If it doesn't have the work of its calling to occupy it, the devil comes and casts in temptation, despondency and sadness," Luther said.

Katherina took good care of Luther's health. As his illnesses became worse with age, she used herbs and massage, natural remedies which were common at that time. Their son Paul, who later practiced medicine, said she was "half a doctor." Medicine, however, had not yet learned what to do for a heart attack. While Luther lay on his deathbed, one of his friends gave him water with powdered unicorn's horn (which was probably the horn of the narwhal whale), while others washed him with lavender and rosewater, but these remedies didn't help.

We know a lot about Luther's family life from daily talks he had around the table, because some of his guests took notes and collected his speeches for publication. The title of this collection is *Table Talk*, and you can find it in bookstores and libraries today.

Besides caring for the large property and its vegetable garden, Katherina kept a beehive and a fish hatchery, brewed beer, and supervised her family farm near the city of Zühlsdorf, about ninety miles from Wittenberg (two days' travel). There, she raised pigs, goats, chickens, and geese. Luther called her jokingly "the rich lady of Zühlsdorf." He also called her "my lord Katie" because she took care of all the daily running of the household. "If I had to take care of building, brewing, and cooking, I'd soon die," he said.

Katherina must have been happy that Luther knew how to sew his own clothes.

He had learned the skill in the monastery. She was less happy when he once cut up little Hans's shorts to make a patch.

❧ In the large monastery that became his house in Wittenberg, Luther built a bowling alley for his students' recreation and played occasionally with them.

❧ Some of the kitchen utensils Katherina used probably included pots and kettles, spits for roasting meat over the fire, and a three-legged Dutch oven to cook whole chickens or ducks. A mortar and pestle were used for grinding salt and spices. Dishes and mugs were usually made out of clay or metal. Most people ate with their hands. Only soups, porridge, and stews required a spoon. For other dishes, it was enough to have a knife to cut the food and some bread to mop up sauces. Forks were considered a tool of the devil because of their resemblance to the pitchfork. Even Luther said once, "God preserve me from the little fork!" Large forks were accepted for serving purposes.

❧ Most of the expenses of the Luther family were for food: many kinds of grains, flour, bread, oil, sugar, spices, fruits and vegetables (mostly peas, cabbage, onions, and turnips), and meat and fish. They also used a lot of tallow and wax for candles. More money went to tailors, shoemakers, belt makers, doctors, pharmacists, tutors for the children, carpenters, and servants. Many products came from the family's properties. One of their gardens included a fishpond so they could have plenty of fresh fish. Luther liked meat. On his forty-ninth birthday, he invited his friends to enjoy a wild boar a prince sent to him as a present. He also enjoyed cherries. He believed they cleanse the head and the stomach.

❧ Luther expressed his love to his wife in many letters. Once he wrote, "I wouldn't give Katie for France and Venice together."

On her part, Katie treated Luther with great respect. As was common in those days, she called him "my lord" or "Doctor Luther."

❧ The symbol of Lutheranism is the Luther rose. It was designed for Martin Luther upon request of John Frederick of Saxony while Luther was staying at his castle. Luther used it as a stamp of approval in his letters. It is a picture of a white rose, which, according to Luther, shows "that faith gives joy, comfort, and peace." Inside the rose is a red heart with a black cross in the center, which remind us of a heartfelt faith in Christ's sacrifice. The rose stands "in a sky-blue field, symbolizing that such joy in spirit and faith is a beginning of the heavenly future joy, which begins already, but is grasped in hope, not yet revealed. And around this field is a golden ring, symbolizing that such blessedness in Heaven lasts forever and has no end" and is precious, just like gold is precious today.

The Luther rose has been used in many coats of arms.

❧ After Luther's death, another symbol for his ideas was the swan. This is connected to some words John Hus said before he was burned at the stake: "You are now roasting a goose (*Hus* meant "goose" in the Bohemian language) but God will awaken a swan whom you will not burn nor roast." We can see the swan in many pictures of Luther and even in Lutheran hymnals. Travelers to northern Germany and Holland are often surprised to see swans used as weather vanes on church steeples and schools instead of crosses or roosters.

❧ In Luther's day, the Roman Catholic Church did not encourage common people to read the Bible. Church leaders thought the common people were not educated enough to understand it and were afraid there might be too many wrong interpretations. Instead, the church encouraged the people to read collections of short biographies of saints with some of their words and prayers. Luther took those books from the churches and replaced them with psalters (books of the Psalms set to music). "For here we find not only what one or two saints have done, but what he has done who is the very head of all the saints," he said. Besides, in the psalter "everyone, in whatever situation he may be, finds in that situation psalms and words that fit his case, that suit him as if they were put there just for his sake."

At the meeting at Worms, Luther admitted that some of his language had not been appropriate. Later, however, he continued to use harsh language against those who were opposing the message of the gospel. In his view, they were speaking on behalf of the devil, so he felt justified in attacking them with strong language. This is not excusable, especially when he wrote against the Jews.

In Luther's day, the Jews were often mistreated because they were seen as enemies of Christ. At first, Luther wrote a wonderful booklet encouraging Christians to be kind to Jews and present them with the gospel. Twenty years later, however, he wrote another booklet and said that Jews spoke for the devil. Initially, he had hoped they would convert to Christ, and when they did not, he became disappointed. This is not an excuse for writing what he did.

Besides books, commentaries, letters, and hymns, Luther also wrote some interesting poetry, including a ballad in memory of the first Lutheran martyrs, "A New Song Here Shall Be Begun." While he was in hiding at the castle, he worked at editing *Aesop's Fables* in German, a book he had loved since he was young.

Time Line of Luther's Life

1483–Luther is born at Eisleben on November 10.

1484–His family moves to Mansfeld, where Luther's father, Hans, works in the copper mines.

1492–He attends school in Mansfeld.

1497–He attends school in Magdeburg.

1498–He attends school in Eisenach.

1501–He enters the University of Erfurt.

1505–He begins law studies. In a thunderstorm, he vows to become a monk. He enters a monastery.

1507–He is ordained as an Augustinian monk.

1510–He visits Rome.

1511–He is transferred to Wittenberg.

1512–He becomes doctor of theology.

1517–On October 31, he posts Ninety-Five Theses on indulgences.

1520–He writes three important documents: *To the Christian Nobility of the German Nation, On the Babylonian Captivity of the Church*, and *On the Freedom of a Christian*. He burns a papal decree of excommunication.

1521–The pope excommunicates Luther. Luther goes to the meeting at Worms but refuses to recant. In May, the emperor condemns him as a heretic and an outlaw. Frederick has him "kidnapped" and hidden at Wartburg Castle, where Luther begins translating the New Testament.

1525–He writes "Against the Heavenly Prophets," "Against the Robbing and Murdering Hordes," and *Bondage of the Will*. He marries Katherina von Bora.

1529–He publishes a large catechism and a small catechism.

1534–Luther publishes the entire German Bible.

1542–His daughter Magdalena dies.

1546–He dies in Eisleben, February 18.

A Portion of Luther's Small Catechism

The Creed

In a very simple way in which the head of a house is to present it to the household

The First Article:
On Creation

I believe in God the Father almighty, CREATOR of heaven and earth.

What is this? Answer:

I believe that God has created me together with all that exists. God has given me and still preserves my body and soul: eyes, ears, and all limbs and senses; reason and all mental faculties. In addition, God daily and abundantly provides shoes and clothing, food and drink, house and farm, spouse and children, fields, livestock, and all property—along with all the necessities and nourishment for this body and life. God protects me against all danger and shields and preserves me from all evil. And all this is done out of pure, fatherly, and divine goodness and mercy, without any merit or worthiness of mine at all! For all of this I owe it to God to thank and praise, serve and obey him. This is most certainly true.

The Second Article:
On Redemption

And [I believe] in Jesus Christ, his only Son, our LORD, who was conceived by the Holy Spirit, born of the Virgin Mary, suffered under Pontius Pilate, was crucified, died, and was buried; he descended into hell. On the third day he rose [again]; he ascended into heaven, seated at the right hand of God, the almighty Father, from where he will come to judge the living and the dead.

What is this? Answer:

I believe that Jesus Christ, true God, begotten of the Father in eternity, and also a true human being, born of the Virgin Mary, is my LORD. He has redeemed me, a lost and condemned human being. He has purchased and freed me from all sins, from death, and from the power of the devil, not with gold or silver but with his holy, precious blood and with his innocent suffering and death. He has done all this in order that I may belong to him, live under him in his kingdom, and serve him in eternal righteousness, innocence, and blessedness, just as he is risen from the dead and lives and rules eternally. This is most certainly true.

The Third Article:
On Being Made Holy

I believe in the Holy Spirit, one holy Christian church, the community of the saints, forgiveness of sins, resurrection of the flesh, and eternal life. Amen.

What is this? Answer:

I believe that by my own understanding or strength I cannot believe in Jesus Christ my LORD or come to him, but instead the Holy Spirit has called me through the gospel, enlightened me with his gifts, made me holy and kept me in the true faith, just as he calls, gathers, enlightens, and makes holy the whole Christian church on earth and keeps it with Jesus Christ in the one common, true faith. Daily in this Christian church the Holy Spirit abundantly forgives all sins—mine and those of all believers. On the Last Day the Holy Spirit will raise me and all the dead and will give to me and all believers in Christ eternal life. This is most certainly true.

From *The Book of Concord* translated by Robert Kolb and Timothy Wengert, copyright © 2000 Fortress Press. Reproduced by permission of Augsburg Fortress.

Acknowledgments

Once again, I am indebted to many people for this book. I wish to thank first of all Dr. Joel Beeke and the RHB staff for their patience with me and their continued encouragement and support. I am also grateful to the people who, in spite of their busy schedules and weighty commitments, have enthusiastically accepted to read my manuscript and to offer their comments: Dr. Robert Kolb, professor of systematic theology, Concordia Seminary, Saint Louis, and author of several books on Luther; Dr. Carl Trueman, professor of historical theology and church history and author of *Luther on the Christian Life: Cross and Freedom*; Dr. Phillip Cary, philosophy professor at Eastern University and author of *Luther: Gospel, Law, and Reformation*; as well as my friends Timothy Massaro and Heather Chisholm-Chait.

A special thanks goes to my Sunday school students Evan Olow, Lucy Plotner, Isaiah Brindis De Salas, Iain Brown, and James, Matthew, Adam, and Olivia Horton, who sat patiently through a reading of this manuscript and shared their opinions and suggestions. As usual, I am also deeply grateful for the support of my husband and children, my friends, and my church family at Christ URC.